What Error Correction Can(not) Accomplish for Second Language Writers

What Error Correction Can(not) Accomplish for Second Language Writers

Dispelling Myths, Discussing Options

Dana R. Ferris
University of California, Davis

University of Michigan Press
Ann Arbor

First paperback edition 2023

Published in the United States of America by the
University of Michigan Press

An earlier version of this material was published as Myth 5 in *Writing Myths: Applying Second Language Research to Classroom Teaching*, edited by Joy Reid (copyright 2008)

First published November 2018

The presentation of tables, figures, and/or images is dependent on the device and display options. Some image content or language characters may have been removed or may be altered depending on the device used to read this ebook.

Paperback ISBN: 978-0-472-03950-0
Ebook ISBN: 978-0-472-12568-5

CONTENTS

Introduction: In the Real World

In 1985, I was a teaching assistant completing an M.A. in Teaching English to Speakers of Other Languages (TESOL) and teaching my very first class of second language (L2) student writers. I worked hard at teaching them grammar—verb tenses, sentence structure, articles, and so forth. I labored over classroom presentations, practice exercises, and tests. I remember struggling nearly the entire semester with trying to get most of the students to write narratives in the simple past tense and to understand that singular count nouns require an article of some sort. At times I thought I was successful—students appeared to understand my explanations and did well on the tests—but then I would receive their next set of papers, and it was as if I had taught them nothing at all! Of course, I also diligently corrected all of their errors so that they would be able to see their mistakes and avoid them on the next paper. Still, progress was minimal.

I took a powerful lesson away from that first classroom experience, one that has shaped my subsequent teaching of L2 composition, my teacher training, my research, and my writing: It is simply not possible to get a whole class of student writers from Point A (wherever they start out) to Point B (perfect, error-free papers) by the end of one writing course. It may not even be possible to get one student writer all the way to that elusive Point B. This insight has led me to think and write extensively about realistic and effective ways to "treat" errors in student writing, focusing particularly on teaching students to self-edit for their most frequent and serious error patterns. The goal is neither to cram students' heads full of explicit grammar knowledge or to try to simply "fix" a specific paper—it is to help students build awareness of trouble spots and strategies for making progress over time.

It is clear that remediating written errors, while not always important, is often important for the goals and aspirations of L2 students. As a young teacher, I was trained to "read past" student errors and focus on the ideas, trusting that over time, errors would take care of themselves. However, I also saw my students have to repeat courses or even have their graduation delayed because of written errors they made on high-stakes timed-writing assessments. While one could rightly argue that such assessments are inherently counterproductive and unfair and that L2 writing professionals should advocate against them (see, for example, CCCC, 2014), there are other, more authentic settings in which L2 learners are also judged harshly because of errors: in written work for other classes; application letters for scholarships, internships, or graduate or professional school admissions; work products on the job after graduation. “Mistakes are a fact of life” (Lunsford & Lunsford, 2008), but errors sometimes do matter, and fair or not, the real world may judge a writer’s intelligence, competence, or effort because of them. L2 writers need to learn to avoid or minimize them, and L2 writing teachers need to help them make progress in this difficult but important skill. We must think creatively and strategically about ways that teachers can help their students to negotiate the gap between what is expected of them and what they may in fact be capable of.

What the Research Shows

Some teachers, as I did early on, persist in the belief that if they just work hard enough teaching grammar, correcting written errors, and holding students accountable for applying the information, they can get students to correct all their writing errors. As a result, they spend too much time and energy on these matters, frustrating themselves and causing stress for students. However, several interacting strands of research provide strong counter-evidence to this belief or myth. Such studies demonstrate at least three "real-world" truths, which we summarize in Table 1.1 and then discuss.

Second Language Acquisition Takes Time

Second language acquisition (SLA) research is quite clear and compelling: It takes years to acquire competence in a second language approaching that of native speakers. When the standard of "competence" is the ability to complete the academic literacy tasks required in higher education, the timeline is even longer.

This observation means that teachers and students are unlikely to succeed in compressing the SLA process into a 15-week course or a single-year immersion program, no matter how hard they try. Rather than envisioning ourselves and our courses as the final stop, we need to perceive ourselves as

Table 1.1: Summary of Research

Observation	Some Key Citations
1. Second language acquisition takes time.	Collier (1987, 1989); Doughty & Long (2003)
2. Second language writers' texts are different from those written by native English speakers.	Eckstein & Ferris (2018); Hinkel (2002); Silva (1993)
3. Even diligent teacher correction and student editing does not lead to perfect, error-free texts.	Ferris (2006); Ferris, Liu, Sinha, & Senna (2013); Ferris & Roberts (2001); Truscott (1996)

part of a process that takes years. To restate the lesson learned from my opening anecdote, perhaps "perfect, error-free papers" is Point Z, not Point B, and teachers need to recognize that if their students move from Point A to Point C, or Point E to Point H, and so forth, they have been faithful in their responsibilities by creating links in a much longer chain of learning.

Because of this reality, L2 writing scholars and experts in writing across the curriculum (WAC) have in recent years called for institutions—secondary schools, colleges, and universities—to take greater responsibility for the ongoing language and literacy acquisition of their students throughout their academic careers, rather than assuming that a pre-admission or entry-level language or writing course will "fix" or even adequately prepare students for all the new challenges they will face over the years and across disciplinary and professional contexts.

This is not to say that L2 language/writing classes are not important or strategic in preparing students for their future courses. They can be very foundational and valuable. However, instructors in those courses need to be realistic about what can be accomplished in a relatively short period of time. Their focus should be on strategies, not end-products, and on progress, not perfection.

Second Language Writers' Texts are Different from Those Written by Native English Speakers

Studies of English L2 writing have yielded a number of specific findings about the characteristics of L2 texts, or at least those composed by student writers in postsecondary classrooms: L2 writers make more errors and different types of errors than do their L1 peers, and they make distinct lexical, syntactic, and discourse-level (e.g., transitional/connecting devices) choices. While numerous explanations exist for these observable and empirically validated differences, the most straightforward one is that, compared with their L1 English-speaking peers, L2 writers have not had equivalent exposure to the patterns of English and especially to English texts—from hearing children's stories to reading college textbooks—that builds linguistic competence and provides a range of lexical, syntactic, and rhetorical tools at writers' disposal as they work.

A related explanation is that L2 students in various contexts have had distinct educational pathways—L2 students have backgrounds that support

L2 learning and acquisition of academic literacy from their experiences as L1 and L2 learners (Ferris, 2009; Ferris & Hedgcock, 2014). Some have studied and learned primarily in their home language (L1), acquiring English only in foreign language classes at school, similar to the way that U.S.-born/educated students may study French or Spanish in secondary school. Some began their education in one language and then, due to family relocation, began learning the L2 later in life, such as in upper-primary or secondary grades. Some grew up in homes in which their parents spoke one language, but their school experiences were entirely in the L2.

These varying pathways have a range of implications for students' language and literacy development. For example, students whose primary exposure to the L2 was in a language classroom may have greater explicit knowledge of formal language features, such as grammatical labels and rules, but have had overall less exposure to the natural patterns of the L2 than students raised and educated in the L2 context. The former group might benefit from specific grammar feedback that builds on formally learned rules, while the latter might just draw on "what sounds right" to correct an error that is called to their attention.

What all of these subgroups of L2 writers have in common is that (a) the amount and types of L2 exposure they have had are likely to be different both from L1 peers and from each other, and (b) they are simultaneously in the process of acquiring not only a second language but also advanced academic literacy, a daunting task. While it may be counterproductive to attach deficit models to L2 writers and to "other" them, it is also unhelpful to simply ignore the different linguistic repertoires and frames of references that multilingual students bring into the classroom (for further discussion of this important point, see Ferris, Brown, Liu, & Stine, 2011; Matsuda, 2006, 2012; Matsuda, Saenkhum, & Accardi, 2013).

Together with the previous observation that SLA takes time, teachers should be reminded that a few grammar and vocabulary lessons are not going to quickly bridge the linguistic knowledge differences. When L2 writers make errors, teachers must recognize that such errors do not simply represent a lack of proofreading or a minor short-circuit that can be fixed with a brief rule reminder, but rather that such errors are often clues about what students do not know about the language system as a whole and about written texts in particular (see Ferris, Liu, Sinha, & Senna, 2013, for a detailed analysis of individual student writers' demonstrations and characterizations of their knowledge of formal rules).

Even Diligent Teacher Correction and Student Editing Does Not Lead to Perfect, Error-Free Texts

The question of whether teacher error correction and student editing is effective has sparked much discussion over the past several decades. In response to some published debates on the topic (e.g., Ferris, 2004; Truscott, 1996), researchers over the decade have completed studies looking at the short- and long-term effects of teacher intervention with regard to students' written errors. Such studies have delivered encouraging news for teachers who intuitively feel that error correction is needed, that it helps students, and that students want it. When error feedback is thoughtfully and consistently delivered, it can help students to improve the accuracy of their current texts (i.e., in revision); growing evidence further demonstrates that effective error feedback also helps students improve in written accuracy over time (for reviews of this evidence, see Bitchener & Ferris, 2012; Bitchener & Storch, 2016; Liu & Brown, 2015).

However, even studies delivering "good news" do not find that students produce error-free texts in response to teacher intervention. For instance, in one large semester-long study (Ferris, 2006), students were able to successfully self-edit—at home as they revised—approximately 82 percent of the errors called to their attention (but not directly corrected) by their teachers. In a controlled experimental study (Ferris & Roberts, 2001), students receiving indirect error feedback (i.e., errors were highlighted but not corrected) in five different error categories were able to self-correct, on the spot, 56 percent of their errors. Now, 82 percent success at home and 56 percent in class are good correction ratios, and they definitely provide counter-evidence to the claim that students do not pay attention to their teachers' corrections or are unable to utilize the feedback successfully when they do attend to it (Truscott, 1996). Yet these student texts were still not "perfect," not "error-free." Most teachers would agree that no error correction method will ever be effective enough to reach the 100 percent standard. Language is simply too complex, and the editing process has too many interacting individual variables for any method or approach to be universally successful in helping student writers to achieve perfection.

In sum, while teachers and their students would like to believe that perfection is possible with the right combination of instruction, care, and effort, that is a myth. It is not, in fact, attainable, at least not in the span of one L2 writing class. Yet, as discussed, not only do teachers and students expect writing to be virtually error-free, but many outside the individual writing classroom hold that expectation as well.

Error Correction in the Classroom: What Can Teachers Do?

So what are teachers to do to help their students bridge that gap between what is possible and what is expected (or demanded) of them? To help students realize that they must take seriously real-world demands for written accuracy and provide them with the tools and strategies they will need, L2 writing teachers must consider several principles and design instructional practices that are consistent with those principles. These principles are outlined in Table 2.1 and then discussed.

1. Give Students Time to do Their Best Work

It is questionable whether anyone can truly excel in writing under time pressure, but this is especially true for L2 student writers. In a multiple-case study (Ferris et al., 2013) of ten first-year college students in an ESL writing class, the students repeatedly explained to interviewers that although they "knew" the rules and could catch errors when they had the opportunity, they simply had neither the time nor the motivation to do so during timed writing examinations because they believed that their argument, organization, and use of sources was even more important to their

Table 2.1: Bridging the Gap: Principles and Practices

1. Give students time to do their best work.
2. Help students understand the importance of taking time to think, write, and revise.
3. Teach self-editing strategies.
4. Hold students accountable for self-editing, and give them focused opportunities to reflect on their progress.
5. Provide expert feedback that focuses on each student's area of greatest need and that moves students toward increasing autonomy in self-editing.
6. Bridge student knowledge gaps through mini-lessons and guided self-study.

overall results and, thus, prioritized them over proofreading. Multilingual students at a different university demonstrated the same thing: Compared to L1 peers, they would make many mistakes during timed writing, but some were quite capable of correcting those errors when they revised those timed texts out of class or wrote other papers out of class (Eckstein & Ferris, 2018).

L2 writing experts strongly advise against the use of "one-shot," high-stakes timed-writing assessments (CCCC, 2014). Sometimes researchers analyze them in controlled studies and sometimes administrators choose such assessments because they are easier to implement and score than more authentic alternatives such as portfolios of student work and/or are perceived as more rigorous or secure (avoiding plagiarism or cheating). It is beyond the scope of this paper to debate such practices, but teachers should be realistic about what inauthentic, time-constrained tests that are produced under pressure truly demonstrate about student knowledge, writing/editing skills, or effort. The truth is that they show us very little that is worth knowing.

Students should be given time and space to write, revise, and edit their work, ideally through multiple-draft assignments that allow them to make several passes through their texts after receiving feedback from various sources (self-editing, peers, teacher, or tutor)—which is, in fact, what all experienced writers do. Timed-writing tasks, if and when they take place, should be primarily for formative purposes (e.g., practicing how to take in-class written exams for future courses), rather than for evaluative ones.

2. Help Students Understand the Importance of Taking Time to Think, Write, and Revise

In addition to structuring our courses and assignments to allow students time to think, draft, and revise, we can teach our students that taking time to write is important. We know that students should not be writing papers at the last minute but composing them over a period of days (or weeks) so that they have the time and distance to reflect on what they have written and notice ways to improve their ideas and expression (language). After all, this is how experienced writers approach most projects. However, as students are usually young and always human, it can be helpful to structure assignments in order to force them out of procrastination habits.

Here are several ways to ensure that students take the necessary time:

- First, give students time to compose and revise their work by including mini-deadlines in each writing assignment. For example, several days before a completed essay draft is due, require students to bring in as homework (or submit to you and/or to their writing group) a preliminary draft of the paper.
- Give them credit for completing it.
- Tell them that their next task is to take that rough draft, read it the next day, and make any corrections to errors that they find, either in handwritten or electronic form.
- Ask them to write a paragraph explaining what they found in their papers and what they learned about leaving time and space for proofreading.

3. Teach Self-Editing Strategies

Depending on their educational backgrounds, some L2 writers have a substantive foundation of English grammar knowledge. Even so, nearly all of them could learn to do a better job of applying the linguistic knowledge they already have to their written texts. This was the flaw in the approach discussed in my opening anecdote: I (wrongly) assumed that students would smoothly transfer lessons learned from exercises and grammar quizzes to their own authentic writing. In reality, most writers need to develop effective strategies to make such connections successfully and systematically. In every writing class I teach, early on I give some version of a mini-lesson on self-editing strategies. It always includes these three tips:

Strategy 1: Reading Aloud

When writers read their papers aloud, it helps them notice missing words or word endings, unnecessary words, and unidiomatic constructions. While not all L2 writers will benefit from this technique as much as would a native speaker with stronger intuitions about what "sounds right," they can still pick up a fair amount from this exercise. Though reading aloud may be a cumbersome activity if student papers are long, students can be advised to break a paper into shorter chunks for editing work, with breaks in between chunks.

Such detailed-oriented work can tax anyone's attention span, so it can be challenging to edit all but the shortest pieces of text quickly or in one sitting.

Sample Reading Aloud Exercise
Ask students to complete a paper draft and print it out. Tell them to read the paper aloud and highlight or mark with a pen any errors they notice. (Alternately, they could save a new version and use Track Changes, Google Docs tools, etc., to mark it.) Ask them to submit their marked paper with a paragraph summarizing what types of errors they found and what they have learned about the benefits of reading a draft aloud.

Strategy 2: Adding Another Pair of Eyes

I always hesitate before giving this advice, as it can seem like giving students a license to cheat. Every writing teacher has stories of students whose in-class work is full of errors, but whose out-of-class assignments are beautifully edited, leading them to suspect that the student's brother or friend has done the work. Anyone who has ever tutored in a writing center can tell stories of student writers who simply want the tutor to fix their errors rather than teaching them anything about reviewing their own work.

Yet if we as teachers see part of our job as helping students learn how to bridge the gap between expectations and knowledge/ability, one important life skill is learning to ask others to help us edit our work. Newspapers and publishers employ proofreaders. Many experienced writers rely on writers' groups, more informal types of peer feedback, or, in business settings, administrative assistants. Thus, we should encourage students to find an extra pair of eyes—a tutor, a friend, a classmate—not only to help them pick up what their own proofreading strategies might have missed, but also to help fill in the linguistic gaps they may have as L2 writers. We should remind students to use their own strategies and not to over-rely on others, because proofreaders may also miss things and because there will be times when they have to operate independently. Further, of course, only writers themselves can ultimately make the final decisions about word choice, phrasing, and sentence structure needed to convey the intended message of the text.

It can be helpful to provide some ground rules to help students understand the line between a proofreader (who points things out) and a copy editor (who actually changes things), such as marking or commenting upon any errors (or other language-related issues) they see but not actually correcting them, and that only the writer can make any actual changes. To enforce these ground rules, if peer-editing is done electronically, the reviewer should use commenting and highlighting tools but not a "Track Changes" tool (as in Microsoft Word®) because turning on Track Changes is too intrusive and/or it is too easy for the writer to simply accept all changes without thinking about their appropriateness or accuracy (or learning from them).

Sample Proofreading Exercises
1. Show the class a sample text or excerpt written by a student at an equivalent level of instruction. Give students time to read through the text and mark any errors that they notice. Debrief what they have found in pairs or in groups and as a whole class with a teacher-marked version. Then ask students to exchange papers they are working on with a classmate and ask the classmate to point out but not correct any problems they see. The partners should have time to discuss each other's findings and have an opportunity to ask the teacher if they are confused or in disagreement about a point. This low-stakes exercise drives home the point that it can be easier to find errors in another writer's work than in one's own.
2. Ask students to take a preliminary draft of a paper they are working on to a campus writing center or other tutor (anyone more expert than they are in English and in writing). Ask them to take notes on their papers about what they discussed and what they learned from the tutoring session and to write a paragraph for you describing and/or evaluating the experience.

Strategy 3: Editing for Specific Error Patterns

As noted in Ferris (2011; Eckstein & Ferris, 2018), certain error types are fairly pervasive in English L2 writing, and some error types are more "treatable" (Ferris, 2006; Ferris & Roberts, 2001), meaning they are at least somewhat governed by rules that can be explained and applied. Examples of "treatable" errors include most verb-related categories (tense, form, passives, modal use, etc.), while "untreatable" errors might include word choices (such as prepositions) and unidiomatic phrases or sentence structures. One helpful editing strategy is to teach students to make separate passes through their texts to look specifically for "treatable" structures/errors one at a time. Many students have found that the advice to look only at a specific structure such as verb phrases or noun endings can be much more helpful than simply, "Read through your paper and correct any errors you might find." Reading their papers and looking only for one error type can be especially empowering if the teacher has already identified specific types of errors as problematic for that particular student writer as she or he learns skills to make progress on avoiding and fixing those errors.

Sample Error Patterns Exercise
Give students a text excerpt that contains a number of easily recognizable errors in a "treatable" category, like plural endings on nouns. Using highlighters, ask them to go through the text and to mark every noun phrase. Then ask them to circle nouns that could potentially take plural endings (i.e., countable). Finally, have them underline every circled noun that has a plural error (missing, unnecessary, erroneous form). Discuss findings as a whole class and answer any questions. Assign students the task of repeating the exercise with a partner's paper or with their own papers.

4. Hold Students Accountable for Self-Editing, and Give Them Focused Opportunities to Reflect on Their Progress

When students are given time and opportunity to write, revise, and edit their work, they can be held to higher standards for linguistic precision in their texts than they could be in the typical timed-writing context. Besides teaching the editing strategies and giving students exercises and assignments to help them practice the tools, teachers should be diligent in holding students accountable for submitting well-edited papers, at least after several iterations of the process. One way to both reinforce the editing strategies and to encourage students to use them is to ask students to write a brief reflection after working on a paper draft about which of the editing strategies they used and found most helpful. A more ambitious approach would be to ask students to highlight subsequent drafts of papers, showing errors they found in an earlier draft and corrected in a later draft.

It is probably unfair to require perfect, error-free writing or to penalize students heavily for errors they make. As already discussed, they are still in the process of second language acquisition, and it takes time. However, it is perfectly reasonable to hold students responsible for making a diligent, good-faith effort at proofreading, editing, spell-checking, and polishing (for word choice, sentence variety, etc.) the final versions of their papers before submitting them for a grade or other evaluation. Every experienced writing instructor knows the difference between a student paper that has been carefully edited and one that has not. In my own teaching, I now build conscientious editing into assessment rubrics for writing assignments, as in this example:

Sample Rubric Item
The paper is effectively edited and shows evidence of careful proofreading (for errors) and polishing (for word choice, sentence style, and punctuation).

5. Provide Expert Feedback That Focuses on Each Student's Area of Greatest Need and That Moves Students Toward Increasing Autonomy in Self-Editing

Teacher feedback on student errors needs to do far more than simply point out what is wrong in a particular paper. Rather, it should (a) help students know from the beginning of the course what their specific trouble spots are; (b) raise awareness of specific language issues through in-text, point-of-error feedback; and (c) move students toward increasing autonomy in finding and correcting their own language problems. Specific suggestions regarding feedback for each goal should be outlined and discussed.

Feedback Strategy A: Identify Individual Error Patterns

Depending on the linguistic/cultural makeup and the English proficiency level of their particular group, students may have varying language problems. I have found that completing an individualized error analysis for each student is very helpful for them and for me in making plans for individual feedback as well as class and small group mini-lessons during the term.

Sample Individual Error Pattern Exercise (illustrative materials are provided in Appendix A)
1. Assign students the task of completing a grammar knowledge questionnaire. I use an adapted version of the questionnaire in Ferris (2014), which asks students about their formal knowledge of specific grammatical categories, their own self-evaluation of their writing issues, and about their usual self-editing strategies.
2. Ask them to complete a short piece of writing either in class or out of class.
3. Then, highlight errors (in various categories; see sample in Appendix A) you see in the text. Do this quickly, without adding any error codes or explanations.
4. Next, review the error categories in class with the students.
5. Then ask them to number each error you have marked consecutively and to log the error into the appropriate category on an error chart. They can ask peers or you or another teacher or tutor for help with charting as needed.
6. Finally, ask them to total their errors in the various categories and list the top three problem areas on a summary form. (Spot-check the papers and charts for accurate categorization.)
7. Ask the students to write a brief reflection about what they have learned about their language knowledge and error patterns and set some goals for the course.
8. Collect the individual forms and compile a class summary form to show the students later. Then you and the students will both know what areas of need individuals have and what problems are somewhat common to the whole class.

Feedback Strategy B: Selectively Mark Errors in Student Papers

On early drafts of student papers, take note of the most important error problems, ideally no more than two or three patterns at once. Along with other issues of content and organization, in a summary note to the writer, identify the patterns (e.g., "Be sure to check your nouns to see if they need a plural ending"). Then highlight instances of errors in those specific categories in the draft. You may wish to highlight all of them or just a portion (a page or a couple of paragraphs, depending on the length of the paper). You may or may not wish to add error codes (pl) or rule reminders (past tense) to the highlighted errors. See Appendix B for a sample student paper that illustrates this error-marking approach.

Feedback Strategy C: Provide Feedback on Shorter Timed Writings

The specific label for this activity is Dynamic Written Corrective Feedback (DWCF), a technique developed by Professors Norman Evans and James Hartshorn of Brigham Young University (USA) that has a growing body of research support (see Hartshorn et al., 2010; Kurzer, 2018).

Though the details can vary a bit depending upon context, the key elements of DWCF are:

1. Students regularly/frequently write short pieces of text in class to a teacher-provided prompt. Typically students are given 10–15 minutes to write.
2. The teacher marks these short texts (usually about paragraph-length), using a standard set of error codes. (See Appendix A for a sample that we use in the program in my department.) The marked texts are returned promptly, ideally at the next class meeting.
3. With the error codes in hand, students attempt to correct as many of the errors as they can. The teacher then marks/scores the revised paragraphs.
4. Students also maintain and update individualized charts each time they complete this process so that over the term, they can observe their progress in reducing errors in various categories.

DWCF provides several important benefits. First, it gives students frequent, timely individualized feedback on their language errors. Second, the task is manageable for students and teachers because the texts are short. Third, it helps students become consciously aware of the different error categories and attend to those that are particularly problematic for each of them. Fourth, students find it satisfying and motivating to regularly receive this specific, detailed feedback and to observe their own progress in real time, via the charts.

Feedback Strategy D: Encourage Student Reflection and Autonomy

If the ultimate goal of treating student error is to help them bridge the gap between the students' still-developing linguistic competence and the expectation of "virtually error-free papers" that many readers outside the L2 composition class hold , then systematically and intentionally moving students toward greater autonomy in finding errors and editing their own work is a critical step. Teachers can build autonomy in several ways. First, in giving feedback, the teacher might want to move from more explicit (all errors marked in the text with codes or labels) to less so (no labels, fewer errors marked, verbal summary notes but no in-text markings) as the course goes along.

Second, as students are taught and then practice a range of editing strategies, teachers can ask them to do more and more of their own self-editing—and teachers can mark fewer and fewer drafts of papers. Teachers should remind students that diligence and attention to errors is expected and will be considered in their final assessment.

Under Strategy A (see above; also see Appendix A), I have provided examples of how students could self-assess their own language needs and set goals at the beginning of a term. Such work can continue throughout a course at regular intervals—for example, students could complete reflections about their timed writings for the DWCF process, or address language issues in reflective process memos submitted with completed papers—and it can be especially helpful for students to be led through some guided reflection about their progress at the end of a course. This exercise provides an illustration of how to approach this.

Sample Reflection Exercise
1. When students do their first timed-writing activity (for DWCF) at the beginning of the course, collect them and make an extra set of copies of the texts but do not return them.
2. Before the end of the term, go through and mark the first timed writings, using the usual error codes.
3. During the last week of the course, return the unmarked timed writings to the students. Ask them to go through and mark and chart errors as best they can, using the knowledge and practice they have gained from the regular DWCF work throughout the course.
4. After students have had time to work through their own unmarked texts, return the teacher-marked ones to the students.
5. Then ask students to write a reflection, using the prompt below (a follow-up to the prompt from the beginning of the course, shown in Appendix A).
Reflection: Reviewing Your Language Goals and Your Progress
Instructions: In the first week of this quarter, you completed some language activities (a grammar test, a vocabulary test, a self-editing activity) and set some goals. In this last week, you have completed more grammar and vocabulary activities. You will have 15 minutes to write. Please write at least one well-organized paragraph about your language goals in this class and for the future. Think about these questions as you write:
• At the beginning of this class, what did you say were your strengths and weaknesses in grammar and vocabulary?
• What were your goals (for grammar, vocabulary, and writing) during this course?
• Did you make progress or improve in any of these areas? Which one(s)? If so, what helped you improve? If not, why do you think you didn't improve?
• Looking ahead to next quarter and beyond, what do you still need to work on in grammar, vocabulary, and writing? What information or strategies from this class might help you to keep making progress?
You might begin your paragraph by stating what your goals were for this class and why you thought they were important. Then add some details (for example, from your test markup and from the in-class editing exercise that you just did). Explain how or why you think you improved (or did not). End by talking about what you can do in the future to continue making progress toward these goals.

6. Bridge Student Knowledge Gaps Through Mini-Lessons and Guided Self-Study

As my first class more than 30 years ago taught me, even the best-taught grammar lessons do not automatically translate into improved texts. Given the realities that our time with students is short and that we cannot fast-forward second language development, our time is much better spent (a) teaching students solid self-editing strategies that they can use for many years to come and (b) providing text-specific error feedback to each individual student in their areas of greatest need. The principles and practices already discussed have explored both types of intervention in some detail.

That said, writing instructors will sometimes feel guilty about neglecting grammar instruction, especially after reading student papers that contain errors. However, without a specific plan or purpose for how and why such instruction should occur, this type of instruction can feel haphazard or artificial, not naturally fitting into anything else the class is working on.

Some brief, narrowly focused instruction on treatable error patterns that is explicitly connected to other editing instruction may be valuable (Ferris, 2011; Ferris & Hedgcock, 2014; Frodesen & Holten, 2003). The final section below briefly discusses providing language (vocabulary and grammar) instruction to student writers for the specific purpose of helping them correct/avoid errors and develop greater language control in their writing over time.

Principles for Language Development in L2 Writing Classes

- **Don't lose the big picture and let a writing class become a grammar class.** There is nothing wrong with teaching formal grammar if that is the purpose of the course. However, if the main purpose of the class is to build students' academic literacy skills—reading strategies; making reading-writing connections; learning about the writing process; understanding and learning about rhetorical situations, genre, and audience—then formal grammar instruction should serve those goals and not be allowed to subsume them.
- **Explicit language instruction should be brief and narrowly focused.** It is much better to go deeply into one topic (e.g., shifting between present- and past-tense verb forms) than to try to cover a broad range of structures in one lesson (e.g., all 12 English verb-tense/aspect combinations). The principles of depth and narrow focus allow the teacher to present models for analysis, explain terms and rules, give students practice opportunities, and make intentional connections between what the class has just discussed and students' own writing.
- **Language instruction should be authentically integrated into other reading-writing class activities.** For example, students could study the grammatical choices made by an author in a text they have already read and discussed for its content/ideas—either to simply observe how a complex structure (such as indefinite articles and the zero-article) works within an authentic text or to notice how the writer uses grammar or word choice to achieve rhetorical or stylistic purposes. Further, when students are working on a writing assignment, the teacher could lead them through a discussion of specific mechanical issues (verb tense shifting in narratives, the use of passive voice, punctuation and syntax within quotations, etc.) that are likely to be relevant for the specific task. Teachers might also design a mini-lesson on common errors made by most students in the class after reading or grading a class set of papers, perhaps using authentic examples from students' own writing.

- **Language development instruction and activities should always include focused application to students' own writing.** It is all too easy for teachers to throw a grammar presentation into a lesson plan and simply hope students remember it later when they are doing their own writing. I once watched a 20-minute lecture on semicolons given by a graduate teaching assistant. It was a well-presented lecture, but it ended with simply, "So, when you're writing—think about semicolons."

It should be obvious that advice to "Think about ____" is not likely to be remembered, let alone effectively applied. Instead, if a language topic is important enough to take up class time, it should be concrete enough for an immediate application activity.

A sample application activity to follow a mini-lesson on shifting verb tenses in narrative writing (based on Ferris, 2014) is shown in Table 3.1. Students could be asked to discuss their findings with a small group, complete a chart, or write a paragraph of analysis.

There are various ways a teacher can build application into a classroom activity or homework assignment, but the important point is to make the effort to do so. Without a commitment to application, the teacher may simply have wasted their own time and their students' time in providing instruction.

Providing or Facilitating Language Instruction: Two Models

Having discussed principles for effective language development, the next question is how to turn those principles into concrete reality. There are two general models, which can be used separately or in combination, to provide

Table 3.1: Application Activity

Find a paper you wrote that includes narrative and/or that describes a text or texts written by another author. Look through that paper and answer these questions:
• Did you shift tenses while telling the story, and if so, did you do so correctly? Are there explicit text markers that show when/why you switched from present to past or past to present?
• Did you use the correct verb tense when talking about the text(s) by another author(s)? Try to explain why you chose to use either past or present tense in that particular context.

language instruction in an L2 writing class in narrowly focused, authentic ways: classroom mini-lessons and guided self-study.

Mini-lessons

As I have written elsewhere (see Ferris, 2011, 2014; Ferris & Hedgcock, 2014), mini-lessons by definition should be brief and narrowly focused. Ideally, they should include these four components:

1. discovery/analysis activities in which students observe the linguistic structure being considered in authentic contexts (i.e., actual sample texts)
2. a focused explanation that might include (depending on the topic) definitions, rules, examples, and tips for self-editing
3. practice activities (ideally that go beyond sentence-completion exercises and ask students to examine the target structure in authentic examples)
4. application activities (as previously discussed)

These components need not always be in exactly this order, and, depending on the topic, each element may be more or less extensive. For example, a mini-lesson on a very narrow point, such as "punctuation of quotations," might involve a minimal explanation section. Appendix C provides one example of a mini-lesson that follows this organizational pattern. These lessons can be delivered entirely in class or can involve a combination of classwork and homework, either in preparation or as follow-up.

Self-study

One problem that many teachers face in L2 writing classes is that not all students need the same information or make the same errors. It can be frustrating for students if teachers spend a lot of class time covering grammar issues that they do not have problems with. A program of guided self-study, instead of classroom instruction or in combination with it, can be a useful way to address this logistical issue. There are several guidelines for making self-study effective and well-focused for students.

- Lead students through an analysis of their language needs and help them to set goals for self-study. The materials in Appendix A, besides providing teachers information for corrective feedback, can also help teachers and their students identify productive topics for self-study.

- Provide students with carefully selected resources for self-study. These may be textbooks, websites, online instructional programs, or simply materials the teacher has developed and made available on a course website or in hard-copy form. The key point is that the teacher should not simply tell students to "go study commas/articles/prepositions/sentence structure" on their own, but thoughtfully match the students with appropriate materials that will meet their needs.
- Create structure and accountability through a graded assignment (could be required for everyone and/or for extra credit). This structure should include deliverables, such as an analysis chart, completed exercises, or a reflective paragraph, to show that the student has adequately engaged with the content.
- Give students opportunities to reflect on their needs and their progress. The reflective activity shown in Appendix A and Feedback Strategy D above provide examples of how this can be approached. Such reflection helps students think concretely about what they have learned and still need to learn, and it promotes autonomy and builds confidence.

Summary: In the Classroom

These six suggestions for "bridging the gap" between what students know and what they are expected to produce, taken together, provide a comprehensive approach to language development and error treatment through the combination of feedback, strategy training, and instruction. The "when" and "how much" of each element will vary depending on the individual teaching context—student proficiency, length of term, hours of instruction per week, course goals—but as an overview, they provide a road map for teachers to design their courses, lessons, and individual feedback interactions with students.

Concluding Thoughts

L2 writing teachers and their students have a problem. Actually, they have two problems. One is that the world outside of their writing classes may be far less forgiving and understanding of L2 writers' written errors, linguistic gaps, and acquisition processes. The other problem is that the teachers and students themselves persist in the belief that if they just work hard enough, students will produce error-free papers at the end of a course. As already discussed, this is a myth—**the issue is not whether students must learn to correct all their errors, but whether they can do this work independently.** However, with the right combination of time, strategy training, feedback, focused instruction, reflection, and accountability, students may leave their writing class with lifelong skills that will help them to bridge the gaps they will face between what is expected of them and what they are capable of doing. If teachers will invest the thought, time, and energy it will take to equip students with those skills, it will be a great gift to them.

Appendix A
Sample Materials for Diagnostic Error Analysis Activities

Instructions: Your teacher has marked the language errors (grammar, vocabulary, or mechanics) in your first-day writing sample. Go through your paper and number every error your teacher marked. Then, for each error, select the error category (type) you think **best** fits the error. Your teacher will explain the categories and error codes. We will use them during the whole course for your in-class writing.

A. Look at your chart. What were the most common error types you found in your paper

____

____

B. What are **three specific language** issues that you would like to improve on during this class? List them below.

1. ______________________________
   ____

2. ______________________________
   ____

3. ______________________________
   ____

Goal-Setting for This Course

Instructions: You will have 15 minutes to write. Please write at least **one well-organized paragraph** about your strengths and weakness in writing in

English and your goals for this class. Think about the following questions as you write:

- What are your strengths and weakness in **grammar?**
- What are your strengths and weakness in **vocabulary?**
- What are your **goals** (for grammar and vocabulary) during this course, and why?

You might begin your paragraph by stating what your goals are and why you think they are important for you right now. Then add some details (for example, from your homework and from your in-class editing exercise that you just did). End by talking about what **you can do** during this class to make progress toward these goals.

Error Chart (for student analysis activity):

Create a chart or table with at least 25 rows (for the first 25 errors marked) and column headings that reflect the error types on which you want to focus, A list of possible categories and codes is provided below, but you may wish to use fewer or different categories, depending upon your students' needs.

Error Categories and Codes (with explanations and examples)

General Category	Code	Error Type	Brief Description	Example(s)
Verbs (V)	**VT**	**Verb Tense**	The time (past, present, future} of the verb phrase is incorrect or unclear.	Yesterday I *drink* water.
	VF	**Verb Form**	The verb phrase is formed incorrectly (wrong or missing ending)	I am *study* engineering at UC Davis.
	SV	**Subject-verb Agreement**	The subject (noun phrase) and verb do not match as to singular/plural endings	Psychology *expose* you to human behavior. One of my classmates *are* sick today.

General Category	Code	Error Type	Brief Description	Example(s)
Nouns (N)	N	Noun Ending	Plural or possessive noun ending is missing, incorrect, or unnecessary	All family *member* are supposed to come to Grandpa's birthday party. We did many *researches* during the summer.
	Art	Article or Determiner	Article or other determiner is missing, incorrect, or unnecessary	I like *that* shoes on the shelf. *A trip* to United States was longer than I thought it would be.
Sentence Structure (SS)	RO	Sentence Boundary—Run-on Sentence	Two or more complete sentences are put together without any punctuation or connecting words (conjunctions)	I left my backpack in your *car can* you bring it to me at school when you go to work?
	Frag	Sentence Boundary—Fragment	A group of words is written as a sentence with a capital letter and a period at the end but is missing information (subject, verb, or an independent clause)	*Although I like hamburgers.* I hate hot dogs He told a lie. *Right to her face.* There were many errors. *Such as punctuation, sentence structures, and word choice.*
	CS	Sentence Boundary—Comma Splice	Two or more complete sentences are joined only by a comma	I hate *writing, I* never know how to get started.

General Category	Code	Error Type	Brief Description	Example(s)
	WO	Word Order	The words in the sentence are out of order according to rules of English grammar	*Especially, I* miss our Spring Festival.
	^	Insert something	A word(s) is missing	A good major helps you earn a lot ^ money.
	~~word~~	Omit something	Unnecessary word(s) here	I chose this major *major* is Because it sounds interesting to me. High school students lack *of* patience to read long books.
Vocabulary (VO)	WW	Wrong Word	The word(s) used do not make sense in this sentence (may be a translation error or a "sound-alike" word error)	At a Wedding, the bride and groom *change their vowels.* The problems were *oblivious.* She always says that raising a pet *needs* a lot of responsibility.
	WC	Word Choice	The word choice is not exactly "wrong," but it does not express meaning clearly or precisely (may be a translation error)	Candy makes children *feel a sweet taste and a happy life.*
	PP	Prepositions	The preposition is incorrectly used in this phrase	I had to be responsible *of* everything.

General Category	Code	Error Type	Brief Description	Example(s)
	WF	**Word Form**	The word is correct as to meaning, but the form is incorrect—for example, using a noun form when an adjective is required	Switzerland is a very *beauty* country.
Various Errors	**?**	**Meaning is unclear**	There are several different errors here and/or the meaning is unclear. Please ask your teacher for help with this.	*He borrowed some smoke.*
Mechanics (M)	**SP**	**Spelling**	Spelling or typing error	I never worried about my *teech* getting bad.
	P	**Punctuation**	Incorrect or missing punctuation (other than comma splices): semicolons, colons, apostrophes, quotation marks, hyphens	When I was in the UK; one morning really freaked me out Student's really enjoy drinking beer. Melissa said, "That Indiana Jones ride was scary"
	C	**Capital letter**	Missing or incorrect capital letter used	Students love to party, *they* also love to eat pizza at their parties. I always do what my *Mother* says

Appendix B
Sample Student Paper with Error Feedback

I agreed with the statement: the reading and writing skills do important role for successful academic life. The reading and writing are connected with every academic life. To learn something new from the lectures, students have to read textbooks or paper, and to express your understating, students have to write down on the answer sheets.

Having the improved reading and writing skills are great advantage to a college students because you can be finished the lots of reading materials for lectures on time, and you can understand better and express your idea effective.

Once the quarter is started, the college students have to read various reading materials. Those could be for their majors or general education classes.

However, the reading materials are sometimes overwhelming amount to read or difficult to **understands depend** on your reading habit. However, if you know the way of reading which has different purpose, you could save your time to read.

For example, my major is engineering. I have several thick text books each quarter.

When I was freshman, 1 tried to read all books, every single page in the textbook. I spent many time to read them all expecting I would get good grades. However, at the end of semester when l got a transcript for this quarter, my grads were not good as much as l expected. When I became a junior year and **get** used to study engineering subject, I understood the way of using the textbooks and studying. Although I spend less time than freshman I spend, my grads were improved.

Secondly, as improving the reading and writing skill, you can understand better and explain your idea in better way. When I took a literature class for general education, I was uncomfortable to read the textbook. The structure of sentences in the textbook was different compared with the major textbooks. The sentences of engineering textbook are normally simple and dear. There are no metaphors and no hidden meaning. However the literature reading had many hidden meaning in one sentence and I had to find the hidden meaning and write the complex sentence about these. The literature class made me awake of the importance of reading and writing skill.

I marked three different types of errors in your paper.

(1) Errors marked in yellow are nouns where the plural ending was either missing or unnecessary.
(2) Error marked in blue are noun phrases where the article (a/an, the) was either missing or unnecessary.
(3) Errors marked in pink are problems with verbs- they either have the wrong ending or the wrong tense (past/present time).

I only marked three examples of each error type. There are others. When you revise this paper and write new papers in the future, try to fix the errors and avoid making new ones.

I also saw some errors with sentence structure—missing words, extra words, or words in the wrong order—and with word choice (a couple of wrong words and a couple of typing/spelling errors). We'll work more on this as we go along in this course, but for now, just be aware that those are issues to pay attention to.

Appendix C

Sample Mini-Lesson Collocations

Words That Go Together

Focus on Prepositions

One of the most difficult aspects of English grammar is collocations. The word *collocation* simply refers to two or more words that commonly occur together to express a particular idea. Consider the following simple examples.

Word	Sample Collocation (+ preposition *or direct object*)	But not...
happy (adjective)	I am **happy about** the Warriors winning the NBA championship. I am **happy for** Warriors coach Steve Kerr.	*I am happy for the Warriors winning. *I am happy about Warriors coach Steve Kerr.
look (verb)	We **looked at** many different couches before we bought one. We **looked for** Steve Kerr at the game but didn't see him.	*We looked the couches. *We looked Steve Kerr.
like (verb)	I **like** *spaghetti.* I **like** *Steve Kerr* because he's a great coach.	*I like at spaghetti. *I like for Steve Kerr.

From these examples, you can notice several things:

- The adjective *happy* can be followed by the prepositions *about* and *for,*
- However, the phrase *happy for* precedes **someone** in particular (a person or a group). If you're talking about **an event or something that happened**, you say you're *happy about* that event.
- The verb *look* can also be followed by a preposition such as *at* or *in.* However, the phrases *look at* and *look in* have different meanings, so if you choose the wrong preposition when writing, you will not express your idea clearly.

- The verb *like* must be followed by a noun (direct object), such as *ice cream, spaghetti,* or Steve *Kerr.*
- However, *like* cannot be followed by a preposition as *happy* and *look* can.

These examples show you two things about collocations and English grammar. First, different words behave in various ways **grammatically**. You must pay attention to how these combinations of words are used (and not used). Second, different collocations express distinct **meanings:** *look at* does not mean the same thing as *look for.* When you are writing, to express your meaning precisely and clearly, you must notice (and research if necessary) how these different little words are used.

In this lesson, we'll focus on two specific collocation issues: How prepositions are used with adjectives and how they're used with verbs.

We will focus on tools and strategies you can use to understand collocations that include prepositions and to research how to use them correctly in your own writing.

Prepositions—A Definition

Prepositions are small function words* that help connect phrases *(prepositional phrases)* within sentences. Some of the more common English prepositions are in the chart. To find more unusual ones, you can search online for "English prepositions."

Single-word prepositions	Two-word prepositions	Three-word prepositions
about, above, across, after, against, along, among, around, as, at, before, behind, below, beneath, beside, between, beyond, by, down, during, for, from, in, near, next, of, off, on, out, over, past, since, than, through, till, to, toward(s), under, until, up, upon, with, within, without, worth	According to, ahead of, apart from, as for, as to, aside from, back to, because of, close to, due to, except for, far from, inside of, instead of, next to, out of, regardless of, right of, thanks to, upto	as far as, as long as, as opposed to, as soon as, as well as,

* Function words" have a grammatical purpose but not a dictionary meaning. Besides prepositions, the other function word categories in English are articles, pronouns, auxiliaries (like may or do), and conjunctions (like and or because).

In English sentences, prepositions begin ***prepositional phrases***, which consist of a preposition followed by a noun or noun phrase, also known as the *object of a preposition:*

- **in** *July*
- **under** *the blanket*
- **after** *John's graduation party*

As we saw in the opening examples, prepositions can follow adjectives *(afraid, happy, excited, interested,* etc.) and **some** verbs *(look* but not *like).*

Collocations with Prepositions

1. Prepositions following adjectives. As we saw above, different prepositions combined with the same adjective can express distinct meanings. Here is another set of examples:

I am **afraid of** driving after dark because my eyesight isn't very good.
I am **afraid of** large dogs when I don't know them.
I am **afraid for** my son, who is in Afghanistan with the U.S. army.

The simple distinction here is that when you say *afraid for,* it usually refers to a specific person or group of people, and you're worried about them, not yourself. When you say *afraid of,* it can be about either a thing (driving in the dark) or a person (or dog!)—but you're worried about yourself and your own safety.

The grammatical rules here aren't especially complicated, but the range of meanings can be a little tricky, as you can see. At the end of this lesson, we'll talk about strategies for using the right preposition after an adjective.

Practice 1 will help you notice how adjectives and prepositions go together in a text.

2. Prepositions following verbs. The rules about verbs and prepositions are a little more complicated. They involve both grammar and meaning. What is the difference, for example, between these two sentences?

1. I **looked for** my car.
2. I **looked at** my car.

Both sentences have the same subject, the same verb, and the same object of the preposition (my car). Only the prepositions *for* and *at* are different. So the grammar is the same, but the meaning is quite distinct. In #1, you don't know where your car is (maybe in a parking garage, for example), so you search for it. In #2, you know exactly where your car is, and for some reason you're examining it (maybe someone hit it, or maybe it has a flat tire, for example). And what about this one?

3. I **looked in** my car.

In #3, the meaning shifts again. Perhaps the car itself isn't what you're interested in (as in #l and #2) but something *inside* the car (for example, maybe you're trying to find your missing phone or wallet).

So, as with adjectives, you must make sure you are selecting the correct preposition to express your exact meaning. However, there are two more grammatical complications with verbs and prepositions:

(a) *Some verbs cannot be followed directly by prepositions.* Take the example of the verb "like" from the chart at the beginning. "Like" is called a *transitive* verb, meaning that it must be followed by a noun or noun phrase *(a direct object).* Other examples include "see" (e.g., I **saw** *the movie;* **I see** *Sarah over* there) or "played" (He **played** *the piano;* He **plays** *soccer).*

(b) Some verbs can function as either *transitive* (must have a direct object) or *intransitive* (can be followed by a preposition) depending on the meaning of the sentence:

- I **ate** *the ice cream* (transitive).
- I **ate** *in the restaurant* (intransitive)

But not:

- *I ate in the ice cream
- *I ate the restaurant

Practice 2 will help you distinguish between transitive and intransitive verbs and examine the use of prepositions with verbs.

Strategies for Avoiding Collocation Errors with Prepositions

Now that we've explained some of the rules and some of the challenges for using prepositions with adjectives and verbs, let's talk about some practical ways you can make correct choices while writing.

1. Be sure that your adjective + preposition combination means what you think it means (or want it to mean). Say you're using an adjective such as "interested." What prepositions "go with" that adjective? If you look up the word "interested" in the *Longman Dictionary of Contemporary English* (ldoceonline.com), you will find that only one preposition, "in," is listed when "interested" is used as an adjective.

You can also simply search in Google or another search engine for "interested collocations." You will get the same result.

However, what if the adjective you want to use is "happy"? If you look up that word using the same tools, you'll find two options ("for" and "about"). As discussed above, you're usually happy *for someone* but happy *about something*. So in your research you need to (a) find out what your preposition choices are and (b) analyze what the differences in meaning are if you have two or more choices. The same meaning distinctions are important for verb + adjective combinations.

2. If you want to use a preposition after a verb, be sure that you're using the right one for your intended meaning (as with the adjectives) *and* that verb is intransitive and can be followed by a preposition. You can say *I looked for my keys* but not **1 looked my keys.* And you can say *I like ice cream* but not **I like for ice cream* or **I like about ice cream.*

You can check whether verbs are intransitive or transitive in ldoceonline.com or other search engines. You will see that "look" is always intransitive (and which prepositions go with it— there are quite a few!). You will see that "like," (used as a verb, is always transitive. But remember that some verbs can be either transitive or intransitive depending upon how they're used (look up "eat," for example).

The **Application Activity** will help you examine your own writing for your use of prepositions in combination with adjectives and verbs.

Practice and Application Activities

Practice 1. The following excerpts are from the reading "Fraud Frenzy..." (Lu & Hunt, 2015).

There are four adjective + preposition combinations in these excerpts. Find them and complete the chart below. Discuss with your teacher and classmates (or think about it if you're doing this exercise alone) why the preposition used here fits better than other possibilities.

1. With the promise of English-language fluency, a U.S. college education is increasingly attractive for many students and employers. And as Chinese incomes grow, more affordable for parents.

2. In China, admission is based on a single test - many are baffled by the need for extra curricular activities...
3. The Beijing Overseas Study Service Association (BOSSA), which was founded to "support excellence and professional standards" among study abroad advisers, says it's aware of the problem of faked applications.

Adjective	Preposition	Other Prepositions That Can Combine with This Adjective (check on ldoce.online.com and/or other search engines).

Using the same website above (ldoceonline.com), find the correct preposition to collocate with the verbs in the sentences below. Find the preposition by looking up the words in **bold**. Be sure to look at the meanings of the different choices! Are there any examples where more than one preposition could work? How would the meanings of the sentences be different depending on the preposition chosen?

1. She worried that her friends would **laugh** ____________ her face.
2. Asking a tutor to correct your grammar errors for you is **frowned** ____________ by teachers.
3. I **study** ____________ UC Davis.
4. My older brother is **concerned** ____________ his grades this year.
5. R.A.s in the dorms are **concerned** ____________ making sure that freshmen don't get into trouble

Practice 2. Look up each verb in the chart in ldoceonline.com. Say whether it is transitive, intransitive, or either (depending on the context). If it is intransitive, note which preposition(s) can follow it. Then write a sentence that uses the verb correctly {without a preposition if it's transitive, with an appropriate preposition if it is transitive). If the verb can be *either* transitive or intransitive, write **two** sentences, using the verb both ways.

Verb	Transitive or intransitive (or either?	If intransitive, which preposition(s) can follow it?	Sample Sentence (write two if it can be either transitive or intransitive)
Buy			
Love			
study			
sleep			
follow			

Application Activity: Examining Your Own Writing

For this exercise, use a paper you are working on now or wrote recently. Analyze at least 2-3 paragraphs or about one page. Complete the following activities:

- o Find and mark every adjective. Do you have any adjectives followed by prepositions (prepositional phrases, as in Practice 1)? For any that you find, check in ldoceonline.com to see (a) which prepositions can go with that adjective and (b) if you think you chose the right one.
- o Look at all your verbs. Are any of them followed by prepositions? If so, check in ldoceonline.com to make sure that verb can be followed by that preposition.

What have you learned about your own collocation choices with prepositions? How can you use research tools to double-check your word choices?

REFERENCES

Bitchener, J., & Ferris, D. (2012). *Written corrective feedback in second language acquisition and writing.* New York: Routledge.

Bitchener, J., & Storch, N. (2016). *Written corrective feedback for L2 development.* Bristol, England: Multilingual Matters.

Collier, V. P. (1987). Age and rate of acquisition of second language for academic purposes. *TESOL Quarterly, 21,* 617–641.

Collier, V.P. (1989). How long? A synthesis of research on academic achievement in a second language. *TESOL Quarterly, 23,* 509–531.

Conference on College Composition and Communication (CCCC). (2014). CCCC statement on second-language writing and writers. http://www.ncte.org/cccc/resources/positions/secondlangwriting

Doughty, C., & Long, M. H. (2003). *The handbook of second language acquisition.* Malden, MA: Blackwell.

Eckstein, G., & Ferris, D. (2018). Comparing L1 and L2 texts and writers in first-year composition. *TESOL Quarterly,* 52, 137–162.

Ferris, D. R. (2004). The "grammar correction" debate in L2 writing: Where are we, and where do we go from here? *Journal of Second Language Writing, 13* ,1–14.

Ferris, D. R. (2006). Does error feedback help student writers? New evidence on the short- and long-term effects of written error correction. In K. Hyland & F. Hyland (Eds.), *Feedback in second language writing: Contexts and issues* (pp. 81–104). Cambridge, England: Cambridge University Press.

Ferris, D. R. (2009). *Teaching college writing to diverse student populations.* Ann Arbor: University of Michigan Press.

Ferris, D. R. (2011). *Treatment of error in second language student writing* (2nd Ed.). Ann Arbor: University of Michigan Press.

Ferris, D. R. (2014). *Language power: Tutorials for writers.* Boston: Bedford St. Martin's.

Ferris, D., Brown, J., Liu, H. S., & Stine, M. E. A. (2011). Responding to L2 students in college writing classes: Teacher perspectives. *TESOL Quarterly,* 45, 207–234.

Ferris, D. R. & Hedgcock, J. S. (2014). *Teaching L2 composition: Purpose, process, & practice* (3rd Ed.). New York: Routledge.

Ferris, D., Liu, H., Sinha, A., & Senna, M. (2013). Written corrective feedback for individual L2 writers. *Journal of Second Language Writing, 22*, 307–329.

Ferris, D., & Roberts, B. (2001). Error feedback in L2 writing classes: How explicit does it need to be? *Journal of Second Language Writing, 10*, 161–184.

Frodesen, J. & Holten, C. (2003). Grammar in the ESL writing class. In B. Kroll (Ed.), *Exploring the dynamics of second language writing* (pp. 141–161). New York: Cambridge University Press.

Hartshorn, K. J., Evans, N. W., Merrill, P. F., Sudweeks, R. R., Strong-Krause, D., & Anderson, N. J. (2010). Effects of dynamic corrective feedback on ESL writing accuracy. *TESOL Quarterly, 44*, 84–108.

Hinkel, E. (2002). *Second language writers' text: Linguistic and rhetorical features.* Mahwah, NJ: Lawrence Erlbaum.

Kurzer, K. (2018). Dynamic written corrective feedback in developmental ESL writing classes. *TESOL Quarterly, 53*, 5–33.

Liu, Q., & Brown, D. (2015). Methodological synthesis of research on the effectiveness of written corrective feedback in L2 writing. *Journal of Second Language Writing, 30*, 66–81.

Lunsford, A., & Lunsford, K. (2008). "Mistakes are a fact of life": A national comparative study. *College Composition and Communication, 59*, 781–806.

Matsuda, P. K. (2006). The myth of linguistic homogeneity in U.S. college composition. *College English, 68*, 637–651.

Matsuda, P. K. (2012). Let's face it: Language issues and the writing program administrator. *Writing Program Administration, 36*, 141–163.

Matsuda, P. K., Saenkhum, T., & Accardi, S. (2013). Writing teachers' perceptions of the presence and needs of second language writers: An institutional case study. *Journal of Second Language Writing, 22*, 68–86.

Silva, T. (1993). Toward an understanding of the distinct nature of L2 writing: The ESL research and its implications. *TESOL Quarterly, 27*, 657–677.

Truscott, J. (1996). The case against grammar correction in L2 writing classes. *Language Learning, 46*, 327–369.